Yoga

For Back
Pain

Monique Joiner Siedlak

OSHUN
PUBLICATIONS

Printed in the United States of America

Second Edition 2018

ISBN-13: 978-1-948834-54-4

Publisher
www.oshunpublications.com

Disclaimer
All the material contained in this book is provided for educational and informational purposes only. No responsibility can be taken for any results or outcomes resulting from the use of this material. While every attempt has been made to provide information that is both accurate and effective, the author does not assume any responsibility for the accuracy or use/misuse of this information.

Notice

This book is not intended as a substitute for the medical advice of physicians. The reader should regularly consult a physician or therapist in matters relating to his/her health and particularly with respect to any symptoms that may require diagnosis or medical attention.

Yoga Poses Photos

Pixabay.com

Freepik.com

Dreamstime.com

Cover Design by Monique Joiner Siedlak

Cover Image by Pixabay.com

Logo Design by Monique Joiner Siedlak

Logo Image by Pixabay.com

Sign up to email list: www.mojosiedlak.com

Other Books in the Series

Yoga for Beginners

Yoga for Stress

Yoga for Weight Loss

Yoga for Flexibility

Yoga for Advanced Beginners

Yoga for Fitness

Yoga for Runners

Yoga for Energy

Yoga for Your Sex Life

Yoga: To Beat Depression and Anxiety

Yoga for Menstruation

Table of Contents

Introduction

There are quite a few positions you can try to get rid of the back but it is always a good idea to stretch and warm up before every exercise.

Tired of taking pain medications for the pains that just do not go away? I think we have all been there where we take a pill for something that never ever works. Anyone one with constant back pains will tell you that whatever they try to do for their pain, nothing ever works. Well, what if someone told you that that the secret for the healing of your pain was inside you all along?

Yoga is one of the more effective tools for helping soothe low back pain. The practice helps to stretch and strengthen muscles that support the back and spine.

After an extensive research, it found yoga to ease the need for any pain medication. While it is never a good idea to exercise let along do yoga if you have severe pain but if you have recurring or chronic pain, then yoga is the best answer for your pain

Cobra Pose (Bhujangasana)

The Cobra Pose is a familiar Yoga backbend. When you perform the Cobra Pose, you stretch the front of your torso and spine.

How to Do

Lie face down on the floor. Extend your legs back, with the tops of your feet on the floor. Stretch your hands on the floor beneath your shoulders. Squeeze the elbows back into your body. Push the tops of your feet, thighs, and pubis powerfully into the floor.

On an inhalation, start to straighten your arms to raise your chest off the floor. Go only to a height at which you can sustain a connection throughout your pubis to your legs. Press your tailbone toward the pubis and raise the pubis toward your navel. Narrow the hip, compressing but don't harden your buttocks.

Firm the shoulder blades against the back, puffing the side ribs forward. Lift through the top of the sternum but avoid pushing the front ribs forward, which only hardens the lower back. Distribute the backbend evenly throughout the full spine.

Hold the pose anywhere from fifteen to thirty seconds, breathing freely. Release back to the floor with an exhalation.

Benefits

The Cobra Pose is best known for its capability to build up the flexibility of your spine. It stretches the chest along with strengthening your spine and shoulders. It further assists in opening the lungs and stimulating the abdominal organs, improving digestion.

An energizing backbend, the Cobra Pose can reduce stress and fatigue. It also firms and tones the shoulders, abdomen, and buttocks, and assists in easing back pain.

Tip

The Cobra Pose will be able to energize and warm up the body, getting it ready for the deeper backbends in your yoga routine.

Bridge Pose (Setu Bandha Sarvangasana)

The Bridge Pose is a beginning backbend that helps to open your chest and stretch your thighs.

How to Do

To begin, lie supine (on your back). Fold your knees and keep your feet hip distance apart on the floor, ten to twelve inches from your pelvis, with your knees and ankles in a straight line. With your arms beside your body, place your palms faced down.

Breathe in, while slowly lifting your lower back, middle back and upper back off the floor. Gently roll in your shoulders. Touch your chest to your chin without bringing the chin down. Support your weight with your shoulders, arms, and feet. Feel your buttocks firm up in this pose. Both your thighs should be parallel to each other and to the floor.

You could interlock your fingers and push your hands on the floor to lift your torso a bit more up if you want or you could support your back with your palms. Keep breathing easily.

Hold this pose for a minute or two and then exhale as you gently release the pose.

Benefits

The Bridge Pose strengthens your back, opens the chest, and improves your spinal mobility.

Tip

After you roll your shoulders under, be sure not to pull them away from your ears. This often overstrains your neck. Raise the tops of your shoulders toward your ears and push your inner shoulder blades away from your spine.

Reverse Warrior Pose (Viparita Virabhadrasana)

The Reverse Warrior Pose is a standing yoga pose which stretches the waist and energizes the entire body. It's usually practiced as part of a Dancing Warrior sequence which moves from Warrior One to Warrior Two and then straight into Reverse Warrior.

How to Do

Begin in Warrior Two Pose. Bring your back hand down to your rear leg, with the palm facing down. Turn the front hand, palm facing up towards the ceiling. Breathe in, extend your front arm up towards the ceiling, palm facing towards the back of the room. Keeping your hips open as you would in Warrior Two Pose, reach your heart up towards the sky. Continue to bend deeply into your front knee; while trying to keep your weight equally distributed on your front foot. Take breaths here for up to thirty seconds, and then return to Warrior Two Pose.

Benefits

The Reverse Warrior Pose strengthens your legs, improves balance, opens the side body, improves spinal mobility, and your core strength.

Tip

It is important that you stay focused on the various points of alignment. Work on getting your leg and feet positioning first. Allow the pose be developed from the floor upwards. Make certain that your front knee stays aligned with the ankle that is in front. Avoid allowing the knee from wandering to the inside. This can trigger a strain in the joint of the knees. Your front shin should be kept vertical. Buildup your stance as needed to make certain that your knees do not move in front past your ankle. You should as well keep in mind that it is not necessary for you to go too far in the backbend. If you feel a collapse or crunching in your lower back get out of the backbend immediately to regain the space in the spine.

Locust Pose (Salabhasana)

The Locust Pose is a transitional backbend that strengthens and tones the whole back of your body.

How to Do

Lying prone (on your stomach), push your chin against the mat. Keeping your hands in fists with thumbs inside, put your straight arms beneath your thighs. Extend your legs straight behind you, hip-width apart. Make an effort with your back muscles and supporting with your fists from below, use your inner thighs to lift your legs up toward the ceiling, raising both your legs up. Keep this position without holding your breath.

Benefits

The Locust Pose opens your shoulders and neck while it strengthens the back and abdomen. It also eases upper-back aches.

Tip

Roll a blanket and position it at the bottom of your rib cage if you're not gaining much lift in your chest. Practicing like this way will help you strengthen your back muscles.

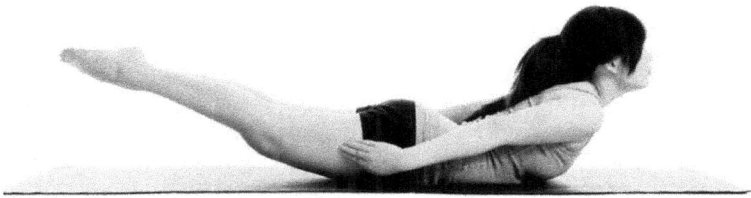

Camel Pose (Ustrasana)

The Camel Pose is an intermediate level back-bending yoga. This yoga posture adds flexibility and strength to the body and also helps in improving digestion.

How to Do

Kneeling on the floor, place your knees hip-width apart and set your hips over the knees. Use a folded blanket if your knees or ankles have aches due to the floor to kneel on. Ground the pose by slightly pushing the top of your feet into the floor.

Lightly tighten your lower abdomen to lean your tailbone down; this will draw your hip points somewhat up towards the bottom of your front ribs. Avoid having stiffness in your buttocks and outer hips while holding this pelvic tilt.

As you maintain a light steadiness in your abdomen, set your hands on the back of your pelvis. The bottom of your palms should go across the tops of your buttocks allowing your fingers to point down. Urge your lower back to lengthen as your tailbone moves deeper into a pelvic tilt as though it is drawing forward toward your pubis. In the course of this action, you should also feel your bottom front ribs slightly being contained as a result adding to the length through your lower back.

Continuing into the back arch, breathe in and roll your shoulders back by pressing your shoulder blades back and against your back ribs. Your chest will inflate and lift. Maintain your pelvis forward over your knees and somewhat lean back against the firmness of the tailbone and shoulder blades.

Remain in this only if you feel relaxed and strong, by slightly twisting to one side to smoothly place one hand on the back of the one heel. Return the spine to center to place the other hand on the other heel. Still keeping the firmness and energy in the abdomen, gently press your thighs forward to perpendicular if the hips have moved back relative to the knees.

Lightly contain the bottom front ribs and continue to lift your hip points towards those ribs to reduce compression of your lower back. Your hands may be positioned so that your palms are on the heels and the fingers point over the soles of the feet. This will allow your upper arm to more effectively externally rotate and add to the expansion of your shoulders and chest. You can continue the pose with the gaze forward. A more advanced version, you can relax the neck and jaw as you gently float your head back. Relax and soften your throat as much as possible-opening the mouth will reduce muscle tension in the front of the neck. Hold the pose with comfort and ease of breath for twenty seconds to a minute.

To release this pose, breathe out and tighten your abdominal muscles. Little by little bring your hands on top of the back of your pelvis one at a time. As you breathe in, tighten your abdominal muscles more to pull your bottom ribs forward causing your trunk to flex forward. Continue to lift your chest over your knees. If your head is back, wait for your chest pass over your knees. At that point let your head flow forward with gravity to avoid strain to the neck. Move slowly into the Child's Pose and rest for a few breaths taking breaths deep into your back.

Benefits

The Camel Pose stretches the front of your body, for the most part, the abdomen, chest, quadriceps, and hip flexors. It improves your spinal flexibility, at the same time as also strengthening your back muscles and improving your posture.

Tip

Beginners very frequently aren't capable to touch their hands to their feet without injuring their back or even their neck. To start with, attempt to turn your toes under and raise your heels. Follow by resting each hand on a block.

Place the blocks just outside each heel, and position them at their highest height. If you're still experiencing difficulty, obtain a chair. Kneel for the pose with your back to the chair, with your calves and feet beneath the seat and the front edge of the seat touching your buttocks. Afterward lean back and bring your hands to the sides of the seat or high up on the front chair legs.

You can also to place a cushion under your knees to assist your way into the pose.

Upward Facing Dog Pose (Urdhva Mukha Svanasana)

Upward Facing Dog Pose is one of the most commonly known, as well as Downward Dog Pose, and recognized yoga pose due to its many benefits and healing uses. Similar to the Cobra Pose, it is thought of as one of the simplest of the back-bending poses and is implemented during the traditional Sun Salutation sequence.

How to Do

Lie face down on the floor. Stretch your legs back, with the tops of your feet on the floor. Bend your elbows and stretch your palms on the floor at the side of your waist so that your forearms are somewhat erect to the floor.

Breathe in and press your inner hands firmly into the floor and somewhat back, similar to trying to push yourself forward along the floor. Then at the same time, straighten your arms and lift your torso up and your legs a few inches off the floor on an intake breath. Keep the thighs firm and somewhat turned inward, the arms firm and turned out so the elbow creases face forward.

Press your tailbone toward your pubis and lift pubis toward your navel. Contract the hip positions. Stiffen but do not totally harden the buttocks.

Steady your shoulder blades against the back and puff the side ribs forward. Lift through the top of the sternum but make an effort not to push the front ribs forward. It will prompt the lower back to tighten. You will at that point look forward or you can angle your head towards the back slightly, remembering to take care not to constrict the back of your neck and the tightening of your throat.

Even though Upward Facing Dog Pose is one position used in the traditional Sun Salutation sequence, you can correspondingly practice this pose independently, maintaining the pose fifteen to thirty seconds, inhaling slowly. Release back to the floor or lift into the Downward Facing Dog pose along with an exhalation.

Benefits

Upward Facing Dog helps open the chest and strengthens the whole body and aligns the spine and invigorates nervous system and the kidneys.

Tip

Performing Upward Facing Dog will elongate and strengthen your whole body. You can use it as a backbend by itself, or as a transition for even deeper backbends.

One Legged King Pigeon Pose (Eka Pada Rajakapotasana)

The One-Legged King Pigeon Pose typically known as the Pigeon Pose is a strong hip-opener that can help increase your flexibility and the scope of motion in your hip joints.

How to Do

Start off in Downward-Facing Dog pose, or on your hands and knees in the Table Pose. Bringing your left knee in the middle of your hands, place your left ankle close your right wrist. Lengthen your right leg behind you so that your kneecap and the top of your foot and toes lie on the floor.

Pushing with your fingertips, raise your upper body away from your thigh. Elongate the front of your body, while releasing your tailbone back toward your heels. Work on aligning your hips and the front side of your torso to the front of your mat.

Drawing down through your front-leg shin, balance out your weight equally in the middle of your right and left hips. Flexing the front of your foot, press down through the tops of all five of your toes and the back of your foot, as you set your focus towards the floor.

Hold this pose for up to one minute. To release the pose, gather your back toes, raise your back knee off the mat, and then push yourself back into the Downward-Facing Dog. Repeat this pose for the equal amount of time on the other side.

Benefits

The One-Legged King Pigeon Pose stretches the thighs, groins, and abdomen. It can regularly be felt intensely in particular upper-leg and hip muscles. It eases tension in your chest and shoulders, as it additionally promotes the abdominal organs, which benefits your digestion management.

Tip

For added support, you may place a thickly folded towel or blanket beneath your hip.

Cat Pose (Marjariasana)

The Cat Pose consists of relaxation of your back by taking on a posture of a cat. It is generally used to begin a yoga exercise, following the initial establishment of breath, by going through cat and cow pose. Amidst a nice steady foundation in tabletop, this movement allows us grounding as we begin to gently open up the back body and stimulate the core. It's most indispensable goal, though, is the opportunity it enables to combine the breath with activity.

How to Do

Start off by placing yourself in a tabletop position, using your hands and knees as the four legs of a table. Your knees would be positioned up and down below your hips. Your shoulders, wrists, and elbows should be parallel and perpendicular to the ground. You will then focus your eyes on the floor, with your head in a middle position.

Let your breath out and allow your spine to curve by directing it upward to the ceiling. Your shoulders and knees should be in the recommended four-legged position. At this moment, let your head somewhat fall towards the floor. Do not fall so far that your chin is pressed into the sternal hollow of your chest.

While inhaling, once again come back to the typical tabletop position. Maintain breathing in and breathing out deeply while transferring your position from relaxed to alert. Maintain until you feel the relaxation in your spine.

Benefits

The Cat Pose gradually works your spine as well as its muscles. It stretches your neck, back, and torso. In addition to improving the functions of your belly organs, it calms your mind by alleviating it from tension and stress.

Tip

The Cat Pose is an easy and simple yoga pose to relax your fatigued body. Ask your partner or friend to lay a hand in the middle of your shoulder blades if you are finding it challenging to bring a curve in the upper section of your back which will then result in a prompt triggering of that area.

Cow Pose (Bitilasana)

The Cow Pose is regularly instructed in sequence with the Cat Pose to do a mild warm-up sequence. When practiced together, the poses help to stretch the body and prepare it for other activity.

You will inhale through the Cow Pose and exhale through the Cat Pose.

How to Do

Begin with your hands and knees in a tabletop position. You should make sure you align your shoulders above your wrists and your hips are aligned above your knees. Come to a horizontal back by lengthening the spine. Place your head and neck in a non-aligned position, staring down in the direction of the floor.

Breathe in and curve your back. Elevate through your glutes and the crown of your head and allow your belly to drop toward the floor. Rotate the shoulders up and down the back, feeling the back bend in your thoracic spine. Widen up your chest.

Hold the Cow Pose for one breath. Exhale and come back to a nonaligned, tabletop position again. You can also practice this in combination with the Cat Pose, alternating inhales with the Cow Pose and exhales with the Cat Pose.

Benefits

This is a gentle backbend that works with the Cat Pose to awaken the spine. Opens the chest, shoulders and upper back. Teaches the connection between inhaling and expanding and exhaling and contracting.

Tip

Care for your neck by widening your shoulder blades and pulling your shoulders down, away from your ears.

Bow Pose (Dhanurasana)

The Bow Pose is an invigorating pose in which the practitioner lays on their belly, grabs their feet, and lifts the legs into the shape of a bow.

How to Do

Lie on your stomach (prone) with your arms by your side and palms facing upwards. Roll your shoulders on your back so that the tops of your arm bones rise off the floor and your shoulder blades move towards each other. Bend both your knees so that your feet move towards your buttocks.

Clasp your ankles with your hands. You can arch your feet to make a handle. You do not want hold your foot itself. Breathe out and tighten through your abdominal area with the principle of lengthening your lower back and bring support to your spine. Breathe in and lengthen out through the top of your head, while, at the same time, maintaining your knees hip width apart, press your feet back into your hands, forming a natural lift.

With each breath, press your heels back and up, gradually increasing the back bend, keeping the spine elongated. Maintain the effective contraction of the abdominal muscles to counter any pressure that may go into the lower spine.

Hold for 5 breaths or more. Exhale and slowly release the feet. Lie quietly for a few moments. You can repeat if desired.

Benefits

The Bow Pose strengthens your abdominal muscles, adds greater flexibility to the back. It tones the leg and arm muscles, opens up the chest, neck, and shoulders and it is also a useful stress and fatigue buster.

Tip

Place a firm blanket or pillow underneath your hip bones for extra padding, if you need it. To prevent ankle, knee, and other leg injuries, hold onto your ankles, not the tops of your feet.

If it isn't possible for you to clasp your ankles completely, use a strap around the fronts of your ankles and fasten the free ends of the strap, as you maintain your arms fully stretched out.

Remember to keep breathing throughout the pose. Do not hold your breath.

Upward Bow Pose (Urdhva Dhanurasana)

The Upward Bow Pose is considered an advanced yoga pose that stretches and opens your entire body. The Upward Bow Pose can be a difficult pose to attain with the correct alignment.

How to Do

Begin in Corpse Pose. Bending your knees draw your heels toward your hips, positioning them as close as possible to your sitting bones. The bottom of your feet should be hip-width apart and pressed against the floor.

Make ready your body for the pose by raising your hips high off the floor. Drawing your back up into an arch, keep your shoulders steadily planted. Your pose should bear a resemblance to that of the Bridge Pose. Keep this pose for a few breaths, maintaining your pelvis and torso raised and your chin up. Drop your hips back to the floor to get ready for the full bow.

Raise your arms straight up from your sides, starting with the backs of your hands, and bend your elbows as they get nearer to the floor. Place your hands on either side of your head, with your palms down and your fingers pointing toward the shoulders. Your elbows should be pointing up at the ceiling, with your forearms perpendicular to the floor. Keep your elbows pulled inward without crowding around the ears and neck.

Press your feet into the floor and again lift up at the hips as you performed earlier. Hold for a couple of breaths. Push into the hands once more, then breathe in and rise to the top of your head, elevating your shoulders off of the mat. Keep your shoulders squeezed into the back but pulled away from your ears. Maintain this position for a couple of breaths in addition.

At this point, push equally into both your hands and feet, breathe out and raise your head totally off of the ground. Straighten your arms as you lift, maintaining your shoulders and tailbone tightly drawn into the back. Lengthen your legs as your arms straighten out up until you reach the maximum height of your back bend.

Maintain this pose for a few steady breaths, increasing from five to ten-second counts if you're comfortable. To release the pose, lower back down to the top of the head. Put your chin in toward your sternum before lowering your hips and torso to the ground to help you prevent neck injury.

Benefits

The Upward Bow Pose aids in strengthening your legs, the forearms, shoulders, and wrists, helps in toning the buttocks and is an excellent stretch for the biceps and triceps.

This yoga pose is also very helpful in increasing the strength and flexibility of your back, spine, and abdomen.

Tip

Your knees and feet have a tendency to spread as you rise into this pose, which constricts the lower back. In the beginning position, you can loop and secure a strap around your thighs, just above your knees, to hold your thighs at hip width and parallel to each other. To keep your feet from turning out, position a block between them, with the bases of your big toes pressing the ends of the block. You'll find that as you go up, you will press the feet into the block.

Half Lord of Fishes Pose (Ardha Matsyendrasana)

The Half Lord of Fishes Pose is a moderate to intense twist that encourages length of your spine, a base stretch for your outer hips, and brings forth growth through the chest and shoulders.

How to Do

Begin in a seated position with your legs straight in front of you. Bring in your knees up and bend them with the purpose of your feet are now flat on the floor. This is your beginning position. Bring your right leg beneath your left leg. Maintain your left leg in the starting position. Your right leg should bend at the knee and then keep close to your hip.

Taking your left leg, cross it over the left knee. Set your left foot flat on the floor on the outside of your right knee. Bring your right arm and reach up. Next slowly bend your arm at the elbow and place your elbow on your left knee. Take your left arm and place behind your back and use for a base.

Breathe in and out while either turning your head opposite to the way your back is stretching, or you can turn your head with your back.

Benefits

The Half Lord of Fishes Pose can restore and improve spinal range of motion. It also beneficial for backaches.

Tip

Maintain your right leg extended if you cannot steadily tuck it beneath your left buttock. Squeeze the left knee with your right arm if that feels better than bringing the right elbow outside the left knee. If you normally use a blanket or other prop under your sit bones for seated poses, it's fine to do that here as well.

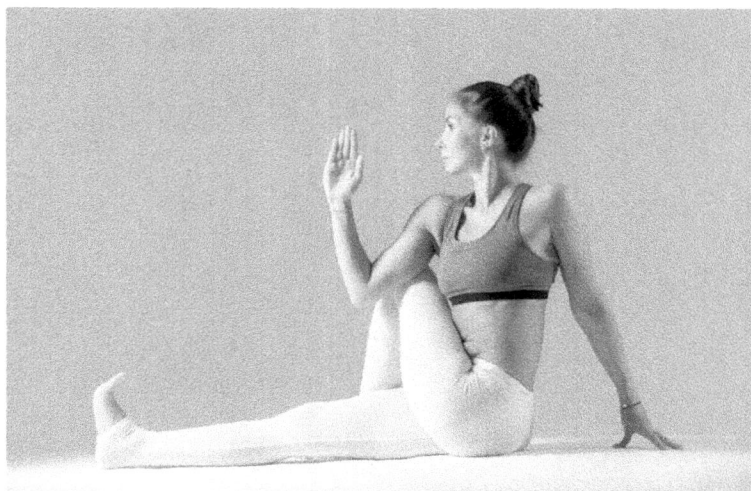

Simple Twist Pose (Parivrtta Sukhasana)

The Simple Twist is a mild spinal twist which is suggested for the beginner to intermediate level yoga students.

How to Do

Start off with sitting in a cross-legged posture on the ground. Extend the length of your spine by sitting tall, breathe out, and then draw in your abdominal. At the same time as inhaling, raise your arms above your head. Afterward breathe out and twist your body to the left while dropping your arms down in step with your breath. The left hand ought to be on the ground next to you, and the right hand on your left knee's outer edge. At this moment, turn your head so you look over your left shoulder.

Stay in this pose for five to ten slow, calming breaths. As you breathe in, see yourself getting taller, and as you breathe out, twist a little deeper into the pose. You should draw your lower spine inwards to the belly, making you sit tall.

When done precisely as suggested, it looks as if the twist began from your pelvis's core and finished at your head. Now twist to the left and lift your arms up as they reach near the center and then again bring them down. Remain in this position for some breaths.

You can then repeat this twist number of times or till you begin to feel its effects.

Benefits

This pose can be adopted for warming up as well as cooling down. Since it stretches the shoulders and upper chest along with massaging the abdominal, it helps with digestion.

Tip

Not advised for anybody with knee problems. Sit up on blocks or blankets if this is uncomfortable on your back or hips.

Downward Facing Dog Pose (Adho Mukha Svanasana)

Downward Facing Dog Pose is one of the traditional Sun Salutation sequences poses. It's also an excellent yoga asana all on its own.

How to Do

Begin with your hands and knees in a tabletop position. Make sure your shoulders are aligned above your wrists and your hips are aligned above your knees. Come to a flat back by lengthening the spine. Place your head and neck in a non-aligned position, staring down in the direction of the floor.

Breathe out and raise your knees away from the floor. At the start, keep your knees slightly bent and your heels lifted away from the floor. Lengthen your tailbone positioned from the back of your pelvis and press it slightly toward the pubis. Alongside this tension, raise the resting bones in the direction of the ceiling, and from your inner ankles pull the inner legs up into the groin.

Followed by letting your breath out, push your top thighs back and extend your heels against or down toward the floor. Making sure that you do not lock them, straighten your knees and steady your outer thighs, rolling the upper thighs inward slightly, narrowing the front of the pelvis.

Firming the outer arms, press the bottoms of your index fingers assertively into the floor. From these two points, lift alongside the inside of your arms from the wrists to the tops of the shoulders. Firm your shoulder blades against your back then widen them and draw them toward the tailbone. Keep your head between your upper arms; not allowing it to simply hang.

Continue in this pose somewhere between one to three minutes. Afterward, bend your knees to the floor with a breath and repose in the Child's Pose.

Benefits

Downward Facing Dog pose can help decrease back pain through strengthening the whole back and shoulder girdle. It aids in stronger hands, wrists, the Achilles tendon, low-back, hamstrings, and calves, as well as increasing the full-body circulation. Elongates your shoulders and shoulder blade area. Decrease in tension and headaches by elongating the cervical spine and neck and relaxing the head. It can also lessen anxiety and expand your respiration

Tip

You can alleviate the burden on your wrists by employing a block beneath your palms or you can be capable of completing the pose upon your elbows. By lifting your hands on blocks or the seat of a chair, you can help to release and open your shoulders.

Seated Forward Fold Pose
(Paschimottanasana)

The Seated Forward Fold is a calming yoga pose that aids to relieve stress. This pose is frequently performed later in a series, when the body is warm.

How to Do

From the Staff Pose, inhale the arms up over the head and lift and lengthen up through the fingers and crown of the head. Exhale and bend at the hips, slowly drop your torso towards your legs. Reach the hands to the toes, feet or ankles.

To deepen the stretch, use the arms to gently pull the head and torso closer to the legs. Press out through the heels and gently draw the toes towards you. Breathe and hold for five to ten breaths. To release from this pose slowly roll up the spine back into Staff pose. Inhale the arms back over your head as you lift the torso back into the Staff pose.

Benefits

The Seated Forward Fold delivers a deep stretch for the whole back side of your body from the heels to the neck. The Forward Fold soothes your nervous system and emotions.

Tip

By no means should force yourself into a forward bend, particularly when sitting on the floor. Extend forward, when you feel the area between your pubis and navel shortening, you should stop, lift up a little, and lengthen again. Frequently, because of the tightness in the backs of your legs, a beginner's forward bend doesn't go very far forward and may possibly look more like sitting up straight.

Plow Pose (Halasana)

The Plow Pose prepares the sphere of your body and mind for a deep transformation.

How to Do

Lie on your backside and bend your legs. While keeping your legs together, set your feet on the floor. Raise your feet and pelvis from the floor. You can assist with your hands, and lower your knees onto your forehead. You can then press your palms against your back or clasp your hands and lower them on the floor behind your back. Go back, rolling your spine back on the floor to release.

Benefits

The Plow Pose opens your neck, shoulders, and back. By compressing your abdomen, it massages and tones your digestive organs, which increases your body's cleansing. This pose promotes and regulates your thyroid gland, helps get rid of excess mucus and phlegm, and regulates your breath.

Tip

With this pose, you may have an inclination to overtax your neck by straining your shoulders too far away from your ears. As the tops of your shoulders should push down into the support, they should be raised toward the ears to keep the back of your neck and throat soft. Open your sternum by compressing the shoulder blades against your back.

Child's Pose (Balasana)

The Child's Pose is a popular beginner's yoga posture. It is generally utilized as a resting position in among more difficult poses throughout a yoga practice.

How to Do

Come to all fours (Table Pose) exhale and lower your hips to your heels and forehead to the floor. Kneeling on the floor, bring your big toes together and sit on your heels, then separate your knees about as far as your hips.

Your arms can be above your head with your palms on the floor. Your palms can be flat or fisted with them stacked under your forehead, or your arms can be at the sides of your body with your palms up.

The Child's Pose is a resting pose. Remain in this position anywhere from thirty seconds to a few minutes. Beginners can also use this pose to get a feel of a deep forward bend. To come up, first stretch your front torso, followed by an inhalation lift from your tailbone as it pushes down and into your pelvis.

Benefits

The Child's Pose aids to stretch your hips, thighs, and ankles at the same time it reduces stress and fatigue. It gradually relaxes the muscles on the front of your body while softly and reflexively elongates the muscles of the back of your torso.

As it centers, calm, and soothes your brain, the Child's Pose is said to be a beneficial posture for alleviating stress. When done with your head and torso braced, it can as well help relieve back and neck pain.

The Child's Pose soothes the body, mind, and spirit while stimulating your third eye. Gently stretching the lower back, the Child's Pose massages and tones your abdominal organs, and encourages digestion and elimination.

Tip

Before you relax completely, press your palms into the ground with your arms straight and elbows lifted. Push your hips firmly back toward your heels. Breathe deeply into your whole back, for an extra release in your back. Make use of this pose to rest in the middle of more challenging poses.

Constructing a Yoga Sequence

Here are a few points to keep in mind how to construct a yoga sequence. You are not at a studio, paying to be there. You do not have to exercise for over an hour. Begin with 5-10 minutes. Notice how you feel by the end of this time. If you feel as if you can do more, go ahead. If no, end your routine there.

Start with 5-10 minutes. By the conclusion of that time, notice how you feel. Do you desire to resume? If yes, continue for an extra five minutes and then check in with yourself once more. If not, close your workout.

The same as any physical journey, a yoga sequence has three clear parts.

Your opening or warm-up sequence

You don't want to jump into the main event tight and cold. This is where you move through and loosening up your major muscle groups as well as body parts

Your main sequence

Once you've warmed up, it's time for your main sequence. This component of your sequence is influenced by the goal of your routine. If it's an asymmetrical pose, keep in mind to do both sides and devote about the same time on each side.

The closing or cool down sequence

Now you've completed the principal portion of your yoga practice, it's time to cool down.

About The Author

Monique Joiner Siedlak is a writer, witch, and warrior on a mission to awaken people to their greatest potential through the power of storytelling infused with mysticism, modern paganism, and new age spirituality. At the young age of 12, she began rigorously studying the fascinating philosophy of Wicca. By the time she was 20, she was self-initiated into the craft, and hasn't looked back ever since. To this day, she has authored over 35 books pertaining to the magick and mysteries of life. Her most recent publication is book one of an Urban Paranormal series entitled "Jaeger Chronicles."

Originally from Long Island, New York, Monique is now a proud inhabitant of Northeast Florida; however, she considers herself to be a citizen of Mother Earth. When she doesn't have a book or pen in hand, she loves exploring new places and learning new things. And being the nature lover that she is, she considers herself to be an avid animal advocate.

To find out more about Monique Joiner Siedlak artistically, spiritually, and personally, feel free to visit her **official website**.

Other Books by Monique Joiner Siedlak

Mojo's Wiccan Series

Wiccan Basics

Candle Magick

Wiccan Spells

Love Spells

Abundance Spells

Hoodoo

Herb Magick

Seven African Powers: The Orishas

Moon Magick

Cooking for the Orishas

Creating Your Own Spells

Body Mind and Soul Series

Creative Visualization

Astral Projection for Beginners

Meditation for Beginners

Reiki for Beginners

Thorne Witch Series

The Phoenix

Beautiful You Series

Creating Your Own Body Butter

Creating Your Own Body Scrub

Creating Your Own Body Spray

Mojo's Self-Improvement Series

Manifesting With the Law of Attraction

Stress Management

Jaeger Chronicles

Glen Cove

Connect With Me!

I really appreciate you reading my book! Please leave a review and let me know your thoughts. Here are the social media locations you can find me at:

Like my Facebook Page: www.facebook.com/mojosiedlak

Follow me on Twitter: www.twitter.com/mojosiedlak

Follow me on Instagram: www.instagram.com/mojosiedlak

Follow me on Bookbub: http://bit.ly/2KEMkqt

Sign up to my Email List at www.mojosiedlak.com and receive a free book!

If you enjoyed this book or found it useful I'd be very grateful if you'd post a short review at your retailer. Your support really does make a difference and I read all the reviews personally so I can get your feedback and make this as well as the next book even better.

www.ingramcontent.com/pod-product-compliance
Lightning Source LLC
Chambersburg PA
CBHW071626040426
42452CB00009B/1503